Fresh, Fast and Fabulous

A collection of simple, satisfying meals from Sam's Club® Members and culinary partners

As a Member, you rely on Sam's Club® to serve up the highest quality foods with a generous helping of value. Our buyers continuously research, source and negotiate with suppliers across the country – and around the world – to bring you exceptional hand-cut meats, superb seafood and fresh produce that's anything but garden variety, all at prices that make truly exceptional eating truly affordable. Even specialty imported cheeses and wines, once the exclusive domain of high-end gourmet retailers, can be enjoyed for casual as well as special occasions, thanks to the savings you receive as a Sam's Club Member.

Inside this book, you'll find a collection of everyday meals and unique entertaining ideas – including creations from the kitchens of award-winning chefs, popular culinary partners and our very own Members. Though the recipes include a variety of products found at your local Sam's Club, most are made with just eight items or less, and all feature simplicity as the main ingredient. We hope you find a feast of ideas, inspirations and new favorites to share with friends and family for years to come. For nutritional information, shopping checklists and more, visit **SamsClub.com/entertaining**.

At Sam's Club, we provide safe, quality food at exceptional savings to our Members. Because we care about your safety, we would like to remind you of the importance of following proper food safety practices. Please visit the Web site below to view safe handling procedures, cooking temperatures and food safety tips for you and your family.

foodsafety.gov/keep/index.html

Consult your medical professional for guidance before changing or undertaking a new diet or exercise program. Advance consultation with your physician is particularly important if you are under eighteen (18) years old, pregnant, nursing or have health problems. If you have dietary restrictions and/or allergies, always read the ingredient list carefully for all food products prior to consumption. Allergens and their derivatives can have various names and may be present in some food brands but not others. If the ingredient list is not available on the food product, check with the food manufacturer or do not consume the product. If you have a food allergy, speak to your physician and/or a registered dietitian for a comprehensive list of foods and their derivatives to avoid prior to using any recipe provided by Sam's Club. Neither the author nor Sam's Club assumes any responsibility for errors, omissions or contrary interpretation of the subject matter herein.

Recipe development on Pages 18, 24, 34, 52, 70, 72, 74, 76, 78 and 80 by Angela Hebert.

Recipe development on Page 28 by Nicole Aloni.

FIRST EDITION

All recipe photography done by Manny Rodriguez Photography, Dallas.
Photographer: Manny Rodriguez
Food Stylist: Erin Quon
Prop Stylist: Jimmie Henslee
Designed and intro written by Launch Agency, Carrollton, TX. Copywriter: Diane Seimetz, **Designer:** Steve Hinckle.

Pictured on the front cover (clockwise from top left): Kaleidoscope Frozen Fruit Pops (Page 114), Caprese Burger (Page 36), Chili-Orange Baby Back Ribs (Page 52), Crispy Buffalo Shrimp (Page 22).

Pictured on the back cover (left to right): Grilled Peach Salsa (Page 28), Southern BBQ Shrimp (Page 62), Balsamic Rosemary Marinade (Page 78), Light and Elegant Salmon Salad (Page 84), Fresh Strawberry Shortcake (Page 98), Sweet Basil Limonata (Page 116).

Printed in China.

Contents

Making it simple:

Fuss-free food prep and storage ideas from the Sam's Club® Kitchens

Give cheese the big freeze: Sam's Club has delicious values on exceptional cheeses from around the world – take advantage of them! Tightly seal in plastic wrap what you don't use. Put in a zippered storage bag, then label, date and freeze. Best to eat within 2 months – thaw in the fridge before serving.

Wine not! Leftover wine after guests have gone home? Pour into ice cube trays, freeze and store in resealable bags for future use in sauces, marinades and dressings.

The time is ripe: In-season produce tastes best, is generally less expensive and travels fewer miles to ship, making it a greener choice. Make sure to visit your local Sam's Club often to enjoy fresh produce – like berries, peaches, plums and apricots – at the height of sweetness.

Give old bread new life: Got a loaf that's less than fresh? Cut stale bread into 1" cubes, spray with nonstick cooking spray and season with dried herbs. Place on a cookie sheet in a 250°F oven until toasted. Instant croutons for salads or as a base for your favorite stuffing.

Take the chill off: Did you know tomatoes and most citrus fruits don't require refrigeration? They taste better and last longer when nestled in a bowl on the countertop.

Read the label: A label maker is a Member's best friend! When repackaging your Sam's Club purchases, an inexpensive portable label maker is a simple way to identify and date foods and include easy instructions directly on plastic bags, plastic containers or foil.

Color keeper: Prevent sliced apples and avocados from browning by squeezing with lemon or lime juice.

Cleaning cookware, easy as pie: Coarse or kosher salt is not just for soft pretzels anymore! Gently scrub salt on the cooking surfaces of your favorite cast-iron and copper pots and pans with a paper towel to remove grease, residue and tarnish. Food-safe, inexpensive and environmentally friendly.

How low can you go: Low-fat or fat-free yogurt makes a light but luscious substitute for sour cream in dips, dressings and most baking recipes.

Encore! Encore! Turning one main dish into a second meal saves time and money. Sam's Club rotisserie chicken, tender roasts and spiral hams are perfect for serving as a main course one night, then creating delicious sandwiches, soups and salads from the leftovers for another meal the same week.

Meet Our Members

One of the things that makes Sam's Club special is our Members. They not only share a passion for quality products at a terrific value, but are generous in sharing creative and tasteful ways to enjoy them. Meet some of the special people whose creativity and tasteful contributions are found in the pages of this book.

Janet Greer

For Janet and her mother, Winnie, family entertaining often revolves around the kitchen – and starts at Sam's Club. From ingredients for made-from-scratch traditions to last-minute morsels, they enjoy the savings and selection. "We never leave empty-handed."

Mike and Debbie Davis
Lotta Bull BBQ

Competing barbecue chefs since 1994, Mike and Debbie Davis know their way around a grill. But whether they're cooking in their own backyard or on the road, they make sure to stop at Sam's Club for supplies. The prices are competitive and the quality is excellent, Mike says. "It's nice to know that I'll always get good stuff."

Lyle Poulson

Like many Americans, Lyle simply has a passion for grilling. He loves to search for great recipes and add his own flair to make unique flavors. His guests then provide the perfect opportunity to test his new creations on trusted palates. They always leave pleased.

Troy Black
Rhythm N' Que

As a full-time barbecue competitor, Troy has had plenty of time to tinker with what makes a great meal. When preparing an award-worthy plate, he demands starting with a perfect piece of meat. To set it apart, he adds the love: his signature rub or marinade, and the proper cooking method.

Rod Gray
Pellet Envy

Rod's daily commute is anything but ordinary. As a professional barbecue chef, he travels the country in search of the next competition and the opportunity to teach others his craft. Whether he's feeding a panel of judges or classroom of barbecue aficionados, quality ingredients are his secret to success.

Jerry Semifero

If it's ordinary, it's just not satisfying for Jerry Semifero. Anyone can cook a hamburger, he says, but when he hits the kitchen he likes to whip up something different. From authentic Italian to Hindu, German and Greek, the food – and drinks – he most likes to prepare has to fit his motto: "If you're going to eat – enjoy it."

Tips, Timesavers and Temps

An easy reference for buying, preparing and storing food.

Tips for Purchase

Chicken

Look for creamy white to deep yellow flesh, never pasty or gray. Check that packaging is unbroken and tightly sealed and has not met the sell-by date.

Beef

The top three grades of beef are USDA Prime, USDA Choice and USDA Select. USDA Prime is the highest-quality grade given by the USDA. It has the highest degree of marbling, which is represented by evenly distributed white flecks of fat. Choice is the second highest grade. It has a moderate amount of marbling and is very flavorful. Select grade has a slight amount of white flecks, with large areas bigger than a dime that contain no flecks of fat. This grade is less tender and not as flavorful as Choice or Prime. Sam's Club® carries only USDA Choice-grade beef or higher for tenderness, flavor and an exceptional eating experience. And all Sam's Club steaks and roasts are hand-cut for guaranteed quality and freshness.

Pork

Look for firm flesh, relatively little fat on the outside and a grayish-pink color. For tender, juicy flavor, meat should have a small amount of marbling.

Seafood

One of the best ways to tell if fish or seafood is truly fresh is by smelling it. Avoid if there is any unpleasant odor or strong fishy smell. Though the product may appear fresh, a strong odor indicates otherwise and will not improve upon cooking. Of course, if you're shopping at Sam's Club, your fresh seafood is guaranteed to please, or double your money back*. Many of our Clubs fly fresh selections in from around the world every day, including ahi tuna, Alaskan sockeye salmon and more.

Lamb

Choose lean cuts with a minimum of firm, creamy white fat. Fat that appears brittle or yellowish generally indicates the meat is old. Adequate marbling, and meat that's not too dry or moist-looking, will yield best results. The New Zealand lamb you'll find at Sam's Club makes an especially good choice, with a rich, yet delicate flavor that's always trimmed to perfection.

Food Safety

Handling

Wash hands prior to handling any foods, food contact surfaces or equipment using proper hand washing procedure.

Wash all fruits and vegetables. If the skin still isn't clean, peel it off. This will help remove dirt, germs and pesticides, if present.

Wash utensils and cutting boards with hot, soapy water after each use. Avoid using wooden cutting boards since they are porous and can harbor germs.

Make sure that food contact surfaces have been cleaned and sanitized before beginning any food preparation.

Before preparing or handling raw or potentially hazardous food, remove any ready-to-eat products from the area to avoid the possibility of cross contamination. If using a ready-to-eat food in the recipe, take precautions to prevent any type of cross contamination.

Preheat cooking unit and allow temperature to stabilize before being cooked. Use only equipment designed for cooking (i.e., not hot-holding units).

Prepare the raw food for cooking as per recipe or other culinary instructions. Begin cooking process when cooking unit has reached required temperature.

*Sam's Club offers Members a 200% guarantee for fresh products (i.e., meat, bakery and produce). We will refund double the Member's purchase price or refund the purchase price and replace the product. A 100% guarantee will be offered to all other customers.

Food Safety, cont.

Cooking temperature requirements vary for different types of potentially hazardous foods.

- Identify the type of food being cooked, and use the chart on page 13 to find the required temperature the food must be cooked to in order to destroy pathogenic microorganisms.

- If a recipe contains a combination of raw products, identify the item with the highest required cooking temperature and cook entire recipe to that temperature.

Storage

One of the great benefits of a Sam's Club Membership is that you can purchase your meat in bulk and then freeze it in the exact portion sizes you'll need for later. Not only does this save you time, but it can also save you money.

Label and date your refrigerator's contents with the purchase date. Leftovers should be eaten within 3 days. After that, freeze for longer-term storage.

If you purchase a fresh product and don't plan to use it within a day or two, freeze it. Bagged chicken, beef, pork and ground beef in a tube can generally be frozen in its original packaging. With fresh meat in trays, remove from packaging and wrap tightly in food-safe freezer bags or plastic wrap. Press out as much air as possible and rewrap with freezer paper or aluminum foil. Freeze fresh chicken, beef or pork if you do not plan to cook it within 2 days after purchase. Once thawed, cook immediately and avoid refreezing.

Do not store raw, over-cooked or ready-to-eat foods.

Never prepare ready-to-eat foods on the same surface or with the same utensils used to prepare raw animal proteins.

Thawing

Refrigerator – Place unopened bag or portions needed (in plastic wrap or in a leak-proof bag) in a large bowl or pan; refrigerate overnight.

Thaw covered, uncooked foods on a pan or plate on the lowest shelf to prevent dripping on prepared foods. Allow a day or more for large items to thaw.

Microwave – Following your microwave manual's defrosting instructions, thaw only a few portions at a time on a microwave-safe plate covered with wax paper. Rotate the plate frequently, checking after each rotation. Turn portions over and re-cover halfway through the defrost cycle.

After thawing, cook immediately. Only use this method if you plan to finish cooking by another process (oven, stovetop) – or continue cooking in the microwave – right after defrosting.

Marinades and Rubs

Marinades are an easy way to add flavor to many meats and seafood, and may help tenderize.

Allow $\frac{1}{4}$ to $\frac{1}{2}$ cup of marinade for each 1 to 2 pounds of meat.

Always marinate in the refrigerator, never at room temperature. Resealable plastic bags are a handy way to keep marinade evenly distributed over meat before cooking.

Never save or reuse marinades. A marinade that has been in contact with uncooked meat must be brought to a full rolling boil for at least one minute before it can be safely used for basting or as a sauce.

Rubs are seasoning blends (dry or moist) applied to the surface of roasts, steaks, chops or patties before cooking. They're great for adding flavor but are not generally used for tenderizing.

Rubs can be applied just before cooking or in advance and refrigerated.

Prep and Cooking Tips

Chicken

Cook chicken to the recommended internal cooking temperature, and until juices run clear.

After roasting, let chicken rest for 10 to 15 minutes before carving to allow juices to be distributed throughout the meat.

Beef

Avoid using ground beef that contains additives or fillers – Sam's Club® ground beef is always ground on-site multiple times daily, which makes it a great choice. Reduce fat in cooked ground beef by rinsing it after browning and before adding to your recipe. Handle ground beef gently; overmixing can result in tougher burgers, meatballs and meat loaves.

Pork

Avoid freezing cooked pork whenever possible to eliminate moisture loss during thawing, which can make meat less tender.

When roasting or broiling, place meat on a broiler rack or roasting pan to allow fat to drain during cooking.

Seafood

A general rule for baking or broiling fish is 10 minutes per inch of thickness at 400°-450°F, turning halfway through the cooking time. Check for doneness frequently to avoid overcooking/drying out.

Lamb

Cuts of lamb with a basic cylindrical shape and even distribution of weight are great for cooking on a rotisserie. Good choices include leg of lamb, rolled shoulder and whole lamb.

Grilling Tips

Brush grates with oil or use nonstick cooking spray before heating to prevent food from sticking.

Chicken

Before grilling, cut into uniform pieces or flatten breasts slightly for more even cooking. Coating with a little oil or marinating will prevent moisture loss while grilling.

Beef

Place 3 to 6 inches away from the heat source (direct grilling method) and cook at medium heat. Thicker cuts should be placed farther away from the heat source (indirect grilling method) than thinner cuts. This helps prevent excessive charring on the outside before the inside is properly cooked.

Turn steaks and roasts with tongs. A fork pierces the beef, allowing loss of flavorful juices.

Pork

Because grilling uses high heat and short cooking times, it tends to toughen pork. Using very tender, marbleized cuts work best.

Lean cuts benefit from marinating before cooking. Chops and steaks that are going to be grilled should be a minimum of ¾ to 1 inch thick.

Seafood

Make a tray out of aluminum foil and place the fish or seafood in it on the grill for gentler cooking and easy cleanup.

To grill shellfish in the shell, such as oysters, mussels and clams, place them directly on the hottest part of the grill. They're done when the shell opens. Discard those that don't open after about 5 minutes.

Grilling Tips, cont.

Firm fish, such as tuna, salmon or shark, can be cooked directly on the grill if handled with care. Skewer shrimp or scallops on metal or water-soaked wooden skewers, or cook in a grill basket.

Lamb

Bring meat to room temperature about 20 minutes before grilling. Meat that is too cold won't cook evenly. Once meat is off the grill, wait at least 5 minutes before slicing, giving the juices a chance to settle back into the meat.

Cooking

Cook foods to the recommended safe minimum internal temperatures listed in the Cooking Safety Chart. Check temperatures with a food thermometer. Learn more about using food thermometers on the FSIS Web site or by calling the USDA Meat and Poultry Hotline.

Cooking Safety Chart

All temperatures are in degrees Fahrenheit

Product	Type	Internal Temperature (^{0}F)
Beef & Veal	Ground	160
	Steak and roasts medium	160
	Steak and roasts medium rare	145
Chicken & Turkey	Breasts	165
	Ground, stuffing and casseroles	165
	Whole bird, legs, thighs and wings	165
Fish & Shellfish	Any type	145
Lamb	Ground	160
Leftovers	Steak and roasts medium	160
	Steaks and roasts medium rare	145
	Any type	165
Pork	Chops, fresh (raw) ham ground, ribs and roasts	160
	Fully cooked ham (to reheat)	140

Source: http://www.fsis.usda.gov/Fact_Sheets/Keep_Food_Safe_Food_Safety_Basics/index.asp

Lotta Bull BBQ Poppers

The perfect popper to spice up your meal.

Recipe submitted by
Mike and Debbie Davis
Marietta, OK
Members since 1997

Total time: 20 minutes | Makes 6 servings

Ingredients:

12	jalapeño peppers
1 cup	cream cheese
½ cup	Parmesan cheese
1 cup	leftover brisket, pork or steak, cut up or chopped
	steak seasoning, to taste
1 pkg.	precooked bacon (1 lb.)
	toothpicks

Instructions:

Cut peppers lengthwise, remove all seeds and veins, and wash. Mix cream cheese, Parmesan and meat together. Add in steak seasoning to taste. Spoon mixture into the hollow of each pepper, wrap with one slice of bacon and secure with toothpick. Preheat grill to medium-hot. Place peppers on wire rack or basket on grill until mixture is warm. Serve immediately.

Dijon-BBQ Sliders

A tangy twist on the big little-burger trend.

Total time: 30 minutes | Makes 8 servings

Ingredients:

2 cups	rotisserie chicken, shredded	¼ tsp.	black pepper
2 cups	shredded coleslaw mix	8	slider-sized hamburger buns or
4 tsp.	apple cider vinegar		dinner rolls, split
2 tsp.	sugar		
½ cup	barbecue sauce		
¼ cup	Dijon mustard		

Instructions:

Mix shredded rotisserie chicken meat with the barbecue sauce and Dijon mustard in a medium bowl until well coated. Warm the mixture in a saucepan over low heat.

In another medium bowl, stir together the vinegar, sugar and black pepper. Stir until the sugar is dissolved. Add the coleslaw mix and toss to coat the cabbage.

Place the barbecue chicken evenly onto the bottom halves of the 8 rolls. Then top the chicken with the coleslaw and the other half of the roll.

Tip: For a southern punch, try adding your favorite hot sauce to the barbecue-mustard sauce. For a southwest barbecue spin, add a slice of smoky bacon to your slider.

Hawaiian Nachos

The islands meet Mexico in this sweet 'n' savory crowd-pleaser.

Total time: 20 minutes | Makes 6 servings

Ingredients:

1 ½ cups	rotisserie chicken, finely shredded	½ cup	red bell pepper, diced
¾ cup	barbecue sauce	¼ cup	red onion, diced
2 Tbsp.	fresh cilantro, chopped	1 cup	Monterey Jack cheese, shredded
½ cup	canned pineapple tidbits	3 Tbsp.	teriyaki cooking sauce
¼ cup	piña colada mix	3	scallions, thinly sliced
6 cups	white corn tortilla chips		

Instructions:

Preheat oven to 400°F.

Drain pineapple and reserve liquid. Marinate diced pepper and onion in ½ of reserved pineapple liquid.

Mix chicken, barbecue sauce, cilantro, piña colada mix and remaining reserved pineapple juice. Warm the mixture in a small saucepan over low heat.

Spread a single layer of tortilla chips onto an oven-proof baking dish. Layer half the chicken mixture on the chips, then sprinkle with cheese. Sprinkle with marinated pepper and onion and repeat to build a second layer.

Bake 5 minutes or until the cheese is melted. Remove from the oven and drizzle with teriyaki cooking sauce. Sprinkle pineapple tidbits and sliced scallions on the nachos and serve.

Bacon and Pepper Jack-Wrapped BBQ Wings

Sweet, smoky, spicy and simple.

Total time: 30 minutes | Makes 6 servings

Ingredients:

24	Tyson® Frozen Fully Cooked Honey BBQ Wings
12	slices pepper jack cheese
24	slices thick sliced hickory smoked bacon
	toothpicks

Instructions:

Soak toothpicks in water for an hour to keep them from burning on grill.

Cut the cheese in half to form rectangles. Wrap cheese around wings.

Wrap one slice of bacon around cheese-covered wing. Be sure to completely cover cheese with bacon. Secure with toothpick.

Grill over medium heat for 13-15 minutes, turning occasionally to make sure all sides are crispy.

Crispy Buffalo Shrimp

A zesty finger-food favorite with a light, baked crunch.

Total time: 30 minutes | Makes 4 servings

Ingredients:

½ cup	hot pepper sauce
¼ cup	butter or margarine, melted
36	Ritz® crackers, finely crushed (about 1¼ cups)
25	uncooked large shrimp (about 1 lb.), peeled with tails left on
¾ cup	Kraft® Roka Blue Cheese or Kraft Ranch Dressing
4	stalks celery, cut into thin sticks

Instructions:

Heat oven to 350°F.

Mix hot pepper sauce and butter in shallow bowl; place cracker crumbs in a separate, shallow bowl.

Dip shrimp in sauce mixture, then in crumbs, turning to evenly coat both sides of each shrimp. Place in single layer on baking sheet sprayed with cooking spray.

Bake 20 minutes or until shrimp are done. Serve with dressing and celery.

Ragú® Pizza Dip

Fabulous flavor without all the fuss.

Total time: 15 minutes | Makes 6 servings

Ingredients:

1 pkg.	low-fat cream cheese, softened (8 oz.)
1 cup	Ragú® Old World Style® Traditional Pasta Sauce
¼ cup	shredded low-fat mozzarella cheese (about 1 oz.)
¼ cup	chopped turkey pepperoni (can substitute traditional pepperoni slices)

Instructions:

In a 9-inch microwave-safe pie plate or bowl, layer cream cheese, pasta sauce, cheese and pepperoni. Microwave on high 1 minute or until heated through. Serve, if desired, with sliced vegetables or bread sticks.

Tip: Can also be baked in conventional oven at 350°F for 20 minutes or until cheese is melted.

Mini-Mexi Nachos

A "poppable" version of everyone's favorite party food that's neat to eat.

Total time: 25 minutes | Makes 8 servings

Ingredients:

1 lb.	ground beef
1⅓ cups	prepared salsa
1 packet	French's® Chili-O® Seasoning Mix
½ lb.	Velveeta® cheese
1	small can black olives, chopped
1 bag	Tostitos® Scoops®

Instructions:

Cut Velveeta into cubes and set aside. Chop olives into small pieces and set aside. Brown ground beef in large skillet, drain fat and return skillet to stove top. Add salsa and French's chili seasoning to ground beef and mix well. Add Velveeta cubes to ground beef mixture and stir until cheese melts. Place a tablespoon of ground beef mixture into each Tostitos Scoop. Garnish with chopped black olives. Repeat with remaining chips. Serve immediately.

Grilled Peach Salsa

Sweet and spicy salsa made easy straight from the backyard barbecue.

Total time: 30 minutes | Makes 6 servings

Ingredients:

3	large, ripe peaches
3 Tbsp.	vegetable oil
3 Tbsp.	chopped fresh mint
⅓ cup	chopped fresh cilantro
¼ cup	minced red onion
2 Tbsp.	minced jalapeño pepper
2 Tbsp.	fresh lime juice
	fresh ginger
	salt and pepper to taste

Instructions:

Slice peaches in half and remove pit. Brush generously with vegetable oil and sprinkle with a little salt and pepper. Grill on medium-high until soft and somewhat colored, 3 to 5 minutes per side. Chop into small chunks. Combine all ingredients in a bowl and toss to mix. Season to taste with salt and pepper (and more jalapeño, if you like it spicy). Serve immediately as a garnish to a favorite dish or as a topper with toasted baguette and cream cheese as shown here. You can also wrap and chill for up to 4 hours.

The Cowboy Steak Show

Recipe submitted by
Rod Gray
Leawood, KS
Member since 1998

Tender, open-faced steak sandwiches with a south-of-the-border sauce.

Total time: 45 minutes | Makes 8 servings

Ingredients:

2 ea.	2-lb. cowboy steaks (bone-in rib eye) approximately 1½" thick or thicker (New York strips or sirloin steaks may be substituted)
2	French baguettes, fresh, cut into ¼" slices
1	head of garlic, cloves separated and peeled
1 cup	extra virgin olive oil

Chimichurri-style Sauce

½ cup	packed fresh Italian flat leaf parsley, minced
½ cup	packed cilantro, minced
¼ cup	fresh oregano leaves, minced
3 tsp.	minced fresh garlic
1 cup	extra virgin olive oil
	salt and fresh ground black pepper, to taste

Steak Baste

2 Tbsp.	cayenne pepper
1 Tbsp.	salt
1 tsp.	garlic powder
1 cup	hot water

Instructions:

Lightly brush both sides of baguettes with olive oil. Grill over medium-high heat to toast, turning once. Cut garlic cloves in half and rub cut edge on each side of warm, toasted slices. This can be done up to a day ahead. Store toasted bread slices in an airtight container.

In a bowl, combine parsley, cilantro, oregano and minced garlic. Slowly whisk in the olive oil – sauce should be bright green and thick. Add salt and pepper, to taste. For best results, prepare this sauce a day ahead – can be refrigerated up to 3 days.

Combine cayenne pepper, salt, garlic powder and water in a squirt bottle and shake to mix. Place room temperature steaks directly on hot grill and baste with liquid as they cook. For spicier steaks, baste more often. Remove from the grill and slice off outer edges of steaks into strips as they reach the desired doneness, returning the remaining steak to the grill to continue cooking. Repeat. Put a slice of steak on the toasted baguette slices and spoon sauce over the top.

Bacon and Bleu Cheeseburgers

Bring home the bacon – and use it to top these savory burgers emboldened with colorful red onions and tangy bleu cheese.

Total time: 25 minutes | Makes 4 servings

Ingredients:

1½ lbs.	ground beef, 85% lean
2 Tbsp.	red onion, finely chopped
½ cup	Hormel® Bacon Crumbles
¼ tsp.	ground black pepper
½ cup	crumbled bleu cheese
4	buns or kaiser rolls, split
	additional toppings: lettuce, sliced tomatoes, sliced red onion, pickle slices, additional crumbled bacon and bleu cheese

Instructions:

In large bowl, combine ground beef, onion, bacon and pepper. Shape the meat mixture into four (4-inch) round patties. Make slight indentation in the center of each patty. Fill each indentation with bleu cheese crumbles. Shape meat up and around the bleu cheese to form a patty. Grill patties on the rack of a grill directly over medium heat to a temperature of 160° F. Cook for 12-14 minutes (for medium doneness), turning halfway through grilling. To serve, toast the buns on the grill. Serve patties on buns with favorite toppings.

Taste of the Old Southwest Turkey Burgers

Lean turkey makes a run for the border in these easy-to-make burgers with a Southwestern kick.

Total time: 20 minutes | Makes 4 servings

Ingredients:

4	Jennie-O Turkey Store® All Natural Turkey Burgers
4	kaiser rolls
4	slices of cheese (any variety)
2 Tbsp.	taco seasoning
¼ cup	sour cream
1	avocado, sliced
4 Tbsp.	salsa (your favorite variety)
	fresh cilantro and sliced jalapeño, if desired

Instructions:

Broil frozen burgers 4 inches from heat, or grill on medium-high heat for 5-7 minutes per side or until fully cooked. Add cheese to the burger during the last minute or two of cooking. While burgers are cooking, combine taco seasoning with sour cream and spread on cut side of kaiser rolls. Top burger with sliced avocado and salsa. If desired, add cilantro and jalapeños.

Caprese Burgers

From the Isle of Capri, a classic burger topped with melted mozzarella cheese and fresh tomato.

Total time: 30 minutes | Makes 6 servings

Ingredients:

Burger

6	Silver T Brand™ or Jensen Frozen Burger Patties
1 Tbsp.	Italian seasoning
1 tsp.	salt
1 tsp.	pepper
½ cup	Parmesan cheese, shredded

Burger Topping

12	fresh basil leaves
12	tomato slices
6	slices fresh mozzarella cheese
½ cup	balsamic vinaigrette
¼ cup	sun-dried tomato pesto (or basil pesto), jarred
½ cup	Parmesan cheese, shredded
6 leaves	lettuce
6	hamburger buns
	olive oil

Instructions:

Put basil, tomatoes and mozzarella slices into a medium bowl. Cover with balsamic vinaigrette and set aside to marinate. Prepare grill at medium-low heat. Grill patties to a temperature of 160°F. For 5.33-oz. patty, grill about 11-12 minutes, turning halfway through, or cook frozen patty 5-9 minutes on one side or until the juices come to the surface. Brush buns lightly with olive oil and place cut side down to toast lightly. Sprinkle cooked patties with salt, pepper, Italian seasoning and Parmesan cheese.

Spread sun-dried tomato pesto on the inside of bottom buns. Place lettuce on bottom halves of buns. Follow with patty. Remove mozzarella, basil and tomatoes from marinade. Top patty with mozzarella slice, two slices of tomato and two basil leaves. Add bun top and serve.

Montreal Steak® Skewers with Tomato-Olive Relish

McCormick® Grill Mates® Montreal Steak® Seasoning and apricots lend a lively new taste to an old favorite.

Total time: 40 minutes | Makes 8 servings

Ingredients:

Tomato-Olive Relish

1 cup	tomato, chopped
¼ cup	pitted black olive halves
2 Tbsp.	balsamic vinegar
1 tsp.	minced fresh garlic
¼ cup	julienne-cut fresh basil
⅛ tsp.	salt
⅛ tsp.	McCormick® black pepper, ground
2 Tbsp.	olive oil

Montreal Steak® Skewers

2 lbs.	boneless beef sirloin or New York strip steak, cut into 1½"-thick cubes
3 Tbsp.	olive oil
1½ Tbsp.	McCormick® Grill Mates® Montreal Steak® Seasoning
2	red bell peppers, cut into 1½" pieces
1	red onion, cut into 1½" chunks
16	dried apricots

Instructions:

For the tomato-olive relish, mix all ingredients in medium bowl; set aside.

Brush steak with oil, then sprinkle with steak seasoning. Alternately thread bell pepper, steak cubes, red onion and apricots onto 8 skewers.

Grill over medium-high heat 8-12 minutes, or until steak is desired doneness, turning occasionally. Serve skewers with tomato-olive relish.

In-a-Snap
Steak and Veggie Kabobs

From flame to family dinner in less than 10 minutes!

Total time: 1 hour | Makes 8 skewers

Ingredients:

2 Tbsp.	Mrs. Dash® Original Blend
1 lb.	beef sirloin, cut into 1½" chunks
2	cloves garlic, slivered
¼	red onion cut into wedges, then in half and separated
1	bell pepper cut into wedges, any color
8	cherry tomatoes
½ lb.	whole button mushrooms
1 Tbsp.	olive oil
	cooking spray

Instructions:

Sprinkle Mrs. Dash Original Blend on meat, garlic, onions, tomatoes, mushrooms and bell pepper. Let sit for 30 minutes. Heat grill or cast iron grill plate to medium-high. Spray with cooking spray. Skewer meat alternately with onion, tomato, bell pepper and mushroom. Brush with olive oil. Grill kabobs about 6-8 minutes, to desired doneness.

Light and Easy Caribbean Chicken

Lean chicken breasts with a fruity salsa that doubles as a dipper with tortilla chips.

Total time: 4 hours 30 minutes | Makes 6 servings with ⅓ cup of salsa each

Ingredients:

Grilled Chicken

¼ cup	Hunt's® ketchup
¼ cup	Worcestershire sauce
¼ cup	white wine vinegar
¼ cup	honey
2 Tbsp.	La Choy® lite soy sauce
2	cloves garlic, finely chopped
6	boneless skinless chicken breast halves

Island Salsa

1 can	Hunt's® tomato sauce (15 oz.)
½ can	Hunt's® diced tomatoes, drained (14.5 oz.)
1 cup	medium red bell pepper, finely chopped
1 cup	fresh pineapple, finely chopped
1	jalapeño pepper, seeded, finely chopped
4 Tbsp.	dried basil
2 Tbsp.	lime juice

Instructions:

Combine ketchup, Worcestershire sauce, vinegar, honey, soy sauce and garlic in large resealable plastic bag; blend well. Pound chicken with meat mallet to even out thickness for more even cooking. Add chicken to bag; seal. Turn to coat evenly with ketchup marinade. Refrigerate 2 hours or overnight. Combine tomato sauce, diced tomatoes, bell pepper, pineapple, jalapeños, basil and lime juice in medium bowl; cover. Refrigerate at least 30 minutes to allow flavors to blend.

Grill chicken about 5 minutes on each side, or until no longer pink in center. Serve each breast with salsa.

Tip: Chicken may be cooked in large nonstick skillet. Spray cold skillet with cooking spray. Place over medium heat for 1 minute. Add chicken and cook about 4 minutes on each side or until no longer pink.

Coca-Cola® Beef Brisket

A favorite for Sunday suppers, tailgate parties and potlucks.

Total time: 4 ½ hours | Makes 6 servings

Ingredients:

2 liters	Coca-Cola® (not diet)
2-3 lbs.	center cut beef brisket
2 cans	tomato sauce (4 oz. each)
1 packet	instant onion soup/dip mix
	ground ginger
	potatoes
	carrots

Instructions:

Place beef brisket fat-side up in a flat roasting pan. Sprinkle onion soup/dip mix on top of brisket, and pour tomato sauce on top. Sprinkle with ground ginger. Pour half of the 2-liter bottle of Coca-Cola over meat. Place whole potatoes and carrots around the sides of the pan. Add enough water to cover meat. Place in 350°F oven for 3½-4 hours, occasionally spooning sauce over meat. If necessary, add a little more Coca-Cola or water to keep the meat covered. Meat is done when fork-tender.

When finished, remove meat from pan and slice fat cap off the top. Using an electric knife, carefully cut meat across the grain into ¼" slices and place in a casserole dish, covering with some of the sauce. Reserve sauce to be used as gravy. Serve with the potatoes and carrots.

Dr Pepper® Beef Tenderloin

Dr Pepper® tenderizes meat and caramelizes during cooking for beef that's sweet, savory and succulent.

Total time: 6½ hours | Makes 6 servings

Ingredients:

2 lbs.	beef tenderloin
1 liter	Dr Pepper® (not diet)
½ cup	soy sauce
¾ cup	lemon juice (about 3 lemons)
1 Tbsp.	black peppercorns
1 Tbsp.	salt
3	cloves garlic

Instructions:

Combine all marinade ingredients in a large plastic bag. Add tenderloin. Marinate for 5 hours or overnight. Heat grill to medium and add tenderloin. Cook about 45 minutes, turning occasionally, until meat registers 130°F. Transfer to board and rest 5-10 minutes before slicing.

Masterpiece BBQ Beef Skewers

A tangy blend of prepared barbecue sauce and fresh seasonings turns meat grill-ready in minutes.

Total time: 30 minutes | Makes 16 skewers

Ingredients:

¾ cup	KC Masterpiece® Original Barbecue Sauce
1 lb.	flank or sirloin steak
3 Tbsp.	minced shallots or green onions
1 Tbsp.	lemon juice
1½ tsp.	grated lemon peel
4	cloves garlic, pressed
16	skewers*
	pepper, to taste

Instructions:

Cut beef diagonally into thin strips about 1" wide. Thread onto 16 skewers, allowing 1-2 ribbons of beef per skewer. In small bowl, combine barbecue sauce, shallots, lemon juice, lemon peel, garlic and pepper. Brush skewered beef generously with sauce mixture. Place skewers on grill and cover. Grill 2-3 minutes on each side.

If using bamboo or wooden skewers, soak in water for 30 minutes before placing on hot grill.

Mustard-Thyme Crusted Rack of Lamb with Pomegranate Merlot Sauce

An easy-yet-elegant company dish from Down Under.

Total time: 60 minutes | Makes 4 servings

Ingredients:

2 racks	New Zealand® racks of lamb

Crust

3 each	shallots, chopped (about ½ cup)
3 Tbsp.	balsamic vinegar
1½ cups	bread crumbs
1 Tbsp.	fresh thyme leaves, chopped
1 Tbsp.	garlic, finely chopped
1½ Tbsp.	olive oil
1 Tbsp.	Dijon mustard

Sauce

1 Tbsp.	olive oil
1 Tbsp.	shallot, diced
1 Tbsp.	garlic, finely chopped
1 cup	pomegranate juice
½ cup	merlot, shiraz or pinot noir
1 cup	chicken broth
1 each	bay leaf
2 Tbsp.	butter
	salt

Instructions:

For the sauce: Heat 2 tablespoons oil in heavy saucepan over medium heat. Add shallots; sauté until golden brown. Add garlic; sauté 3 minutes, being careful not to burn the garlic. Add the red wine and reduce until most of liquid evaporates. Add chicken broth, pomegranate juice and bay leaf; reduce to 1 cup, strain and set aside.

For the crust: In a small sauté pan, heat oil over moderate heat until hot but not smoking and cook shallots, about 3 minutes. Add garlic; stir. Then add vinegar and bring mixture to a boil. Remove pan from heat and allow to cool slightly, then stir in bread crumbs, thyme and adjust salt and pepper if needed.

For the lamb: Preheat oven to 375°F. Season lamb with salt and pepper and arrange, ribs side down, in a small roasting pan. Spread meat side with mustard and pat on crumb mixture evenly. Roast lamb in middle of oven until meat registers 130–135°F for medium-rare, 25–30 minutes.

To serve: When lamb reaches desired temperature, carefully transfer to a cutting board, tent with foil and let stand 5 to 10 minutes. (Lamb will continue to rise in temperature approximately 5°F.)

Bring reduction to a low simmer and gradually whisk in butter until incorporated, being careful not to overheat sauce for the butter will separate. Slice lamb into chops and serve with sauce.

Chili-Orange Baby Back Ribs

Tender pork ribs with a kick of citrus and chili.

Total time: 3 hours | Makes 4 servings

Ingredients:

4 lbs.	baby back pork ribs
1½ cup	orange juice
½ cup	chili sauce
2 Tbsp.	hoisin sauce
1 Tbsp.	orange rind, grated
1 Tbsp.	hot sauce (or to taste)
2 tsp.	brown sugar, firmly packed

Instructions:

Place ribs in a 4- to 5-quart dish. Add orange juice and cover. Marinate 30–60 minutes. Combine chili sauce, hoisin sauce, orange rind, hot sauce and brown sugar in a small bowl. Prepare a medium fire in charcoal grill or preheat one side of grill to medium. Remove ribs from dish and pat dry. Place ribs on grill and grill with indirect heat about 1½–2 hours or until tender, brushing with sauce several times during the last 20 minutes of grilling.

SoCal Spinach Veggie Burger

Prepared spinach dip is the secret sauce on this meatless main dish.

Total time: 30 minutes | Makes 6 servings

Ingredients:

6	frozen veggie burger patties
½ cup	prepared spinach dip
1 cup	baby spinach leaves
6	provolone cheese slices
12	tomato slices
3	avocados, peeled and sliced
¾ cup	alfalfa sprouts
6	hamburger buns
¼ cup	olive oil

Instructions:

Peel and slice avocados. Slice tomatoes and wash spinach and alfalfa sprouts. Prepare grill at medium-high heat. Grill patties from frozen to a temperature of 160°F, about 5 minutes on each side. Melt cheese on patty prior to removing from grill. Brush buns lightly with oil and place cut side down on grill to toast lightly. Spread spinach dip on the inside of buns. Place baby spinach on bottom halves of buns. Follow with patty. Top patty with two slices of tomato, avocado slices and ⅛ cup of sprouts. Add bun top and serve.

Tangy Mahi-Mahi Tacos

Flavorful fish tacos with fresh fruit, spices and a touch of cool sour cream.

Total time: 20 minutes | Makes 4 servings

Ingredients:

4	mahi-mahi fillets, thawed
½ cup	sour cream
½ tsp.	chili powder
½ tsp.	cumin
1	lime, juiced
1	mango, peeled and cubed
½	red or sweet white onion, finely chopped
1	avocado, peeled and diced
1	garlic clove, finely minced
1 cup	fresh cilantro, chopped
1	jalapeño, seeded and finely minced
	whole wheat flour tortillas
	olive oil
	salt and pepper to taste
	shredded lettuce
	chopped tomato

Instructions:

Brush both sides of thawed mahi-mahi fillets with olive oil and sprinkle with salt and pepper, to taste. Grill fillets over medium heat for 3-4 minutes per side, or until they are no longer translucent in the center. Fish is done when it flakes when tested with a fork.

While the fish is grilling, combine sour cream, chili powder, cumin and half the lime juice; set aside. In a separate bowl, gently toss the mango, avocado, onion, garlic, jalapeño and cilantro with the remaining lime juice.

Place cooked mahi-mahi in a warm tortilla. Add mango salsa, lettuce and tomato. Drizzle with the sour cream mixture. Serve with Spanish rice and fresh grilled pineapple skewers.

Tip: Place aluminum foil on the grill to prevent fish from sticking.

A.1.® Chipotle Steak

Piquant peppers and this ever-popular steak sauce create a meal that's A1 with friends and family.

Total time: 55 minutes | Makes 8 servings, ½ steak each

Ingredients:

¾ cup   A.1.® Original Steak Sauce
4   boneless beef ribeye steaks (8 oz. each)
2 Tbsp. lime juice
3 Tbsp. chipotle peppers in adobo sauce, chopped and divided
⅓ cup   butter, softened

Instructions:

Mix steak sauce, lime juice and 1 tablespoon of the chipotle peppers until well blended. Remove ½ cup of the steak sauce mixture for brushing onto steaks as they cook. Pour remaining steak sauce mixture over steaks in large resealable plastic bag; seal bag. Turn bag over several times to evenly coat steaks. Refrigerate 30 minutes to marinate.

Meanwhile, mix butter and remaining 2 tablespoons chipotle peppers until well blended; cover. Refrigerate until ready to use. Preheat grill to medium heat. Remove steaks from marinade; discard bag and marinade. Grill steaks 8–10 minutes for medium-rare to medium doneness, turning occasionally and brushing with the reserved steak sauce mixture. Remove steaks from grill; cut in half. Top with the butter mixture before serving.

Seared Ahi Tuna Steaks

A medley of fresh flavors that will please your palate.

Total time: 1 hour 20 minutes | Makes 4 servings

Ingredients:

4	ahi tuna steaks, thawed
1 Tbsp.	rice vinegar
½ cup	soy sauce
¼ cup	orange juice
¼ cup	lemon juice
1	orange, peeled, sectioned and diced
1	grapefruit, peeled, sectioned and diced

1	jalapeño, seeded and diced
1 cup	cilantro, chopped
1	bunch scallions, chopped
1 lb.	fresh asparagus spears, trimmed
1 Tbsp.	olive oil
	salt and pepper to taste

Instructions:

Combine rice vinegar, soy sauce, orange juice and lemon juice to create marinade. Place tuna steaks in a shallow glass dish and cover with marinade. Cover dish with plastic wrap and marinate tuna steaks in the refrigerator for 1 hour.

Peel, section and dice the orange and grapefruit. Combine with the jalapeño, cilantro and scallions. Set aside.

Grill the marinated tuna steaks 2-3 minutes per side over high heat, depending on how rare you like your steaks. For rare, cook for 4 minutes total. For medium, cook for 5 minutes total. For well done, cook for 6 minutes total.

Toss asparagus with olive oil and season with salt and pepper. Grill 2-4 minutes, or to desired tenderness. Diagonally slice the tuna into ¼"-thick slices and serve over the grilled asparagus. Top tuna with the citrus salad.

Southern BBQ Shrimp

Sunny and savory with a hint of sweetness.

Total time: 6½ hours | Makes 20 skewers

Ingredients:

2 lbs.	uncooked jumbo shrimp, thawed
1 cup	unsalted butter, melted (2 sticks)
½ cup	Worcestershire sauce
½ cup	fresh lemon juice
1 Tbsp.	lemon zest
3 Tbsp.	golden brown sugar, packed
5 Tbsp.	Old Bay® seasoning

Instructions:

Preheat grill to medium-high heat.

Combine butter, Worcestershire sauce, lemon juice and zest, brown sugar and Old Bay in a large mixing bowl and stir well. Separate into 2 portions and set aside.

Thread shrimp onto skewers and place in a large flat baking dish or one-gallon resealable plastic bag.

Pour one half of the marinade over skewered shrimp and cover (or seal in bag). Let sit in the refrigerator for at least 20 minutes or 4-6 hours.

Place skewers on hot grill and cook 2–3 minutes on each side.

Arrange shrimp on a serving platter and drizzle with the remaining marinade. Garnish with lemon wedges and crispy baguette slices.

Samuel Adams Boston Lager® Steak Tacos

Brew-marinated skirt steak makes traditional tacos into fiesta fare.

Total time: 4 hours 10 minutes | Makes 12 servings

Ingredients:

12 oz.	Samuel Adams Boston Lager®	2	limes, quartered
2 lbs.	skirt steak, trimmed	1	red onion, sliced
12 oz.	Coca-Cola® (not diet)	1 bunch	cilantro, chopped
3	cloves garlic	24	corn tortillas
1	onion	1 lb.	Monterey Jack cheese, shredded
2 Tbsp.	soy sauce		prepared guacamole
	salt and pepper		

Instructions:

Combine the following ingredients in blender container and puree until smooth: Sam Adams Boston Lager, Coca-Cola, garlic, onion and soy sauce. Then pour mixture over skirt steak and let marinate at least 4 hours, preferably overnight. Lightly grill on medium heat.

Dry steak and season with salt and pepper. Discard excess marinade. Grill to medium-rare. Set aside and slice across grain. Heat tortillas for 30 seconds on grill. Top with cheese, guacamole, steak, sliced onions and cilantro. Serve with limes.

Hawaiian Chicken Sandwich

Create your own luau with island-inspired flavors in this tropical chicken sandwich.

Total time: 4 ½ hours | Makes 8 servings

Ingredients:

8   boneless, skinless chicken breasts (5-6 oz.)

Marinade:

1 cup	vegetable oil	1 tsp.	onion powder
1 cup	brown sugar	16	canned pineapple slices
1 cup	soy sauce	8	slices Swiss cheese
2 Tbsp.	garlic, minced	8	Sandwich Thins® rolls
2 cups	pineapple juice	8	lettuce leaves
1 tsp.	fresh ginger	8	tomato slices

Instructions:

Cover chicken with plastic wrap and flatten with mallet to about ½" thickness. In a small bowl, combine marinade ingredients. Place chicken in a container and cover with 3 cups of marinade. Cover and chill in refrigerator for 4 hours. Place pineapple slices in another container and add 1 cup of marinade. Cover and chill in refrigerator for 4 hours. Any remaining marinade can be heated on the stove top for 10 minutes over medium heat until thick and used for sauce on burger.

Preheat grill to medium heat. Remove chicken from marinade and discard marinade. Grill over medium heat for 4-6 minutes per side to 165°F. Remove pineapple from marinade, place on grill over medium heat and cook 2-4 minutes on each side. About 1 minute prior to removing the chicken from the grill, place a slice of Swiss cheese on top of each chicken breast and cook until melted.

Brush Sandwich Thins rolls lightly with oil and place cut side down to toast lightly. Spread the teriyaki glaze that was heated from the remaining marinade on the inside of buns. Place lettuce on bottom halves of buns. Follow with chicken. Top chicken with sliced tomatoes and grilled pineapple. Add bun top and serve.

Tip: To save time you can also use a prepared, store-bought teriyaki marinade.

Georgia Peach BBQ Chicken

Serve with grilled fresh peaches to add a touch of summer sweetness to your meal.

Total time: 30 minutes | Makes 4 servings

Ingredients:

4	Tyson® boneless, skinless chicken breasts
2 tsp.	onion salt
⅓ cup	peach preserves
3 Tbsp.	barbecue sauce
4	fresh peaches, grilled (optional)

Instructions:

Preheat grill to medium. Sprinkle chicken with 1 teaspoon onion salt. Combine peach preserves, barbecue sauce and remaining 1 teaspoon onion salt in a small bowl.

Grill chicken, turning and brushing frequently with peach-barbecue sauce, for 15–20 minutes or until done (170°F).

Tip: For a special topping, add grilled fresh peaches to your chicken. Prepare by cutting fresh peaches in half and removing stone. Brush with oil or a light brushing of peach preserves. Grill fruit, cut side down, for about 5 minutes, or until the fruit is slightly soft and well marked.

BEEF AND PORK

Recipes submitted by
Troy Black
Birmingham, AL
Member since 2007

SAUCE
Sweet 'n' Smoky Brisket Sauce
Total time: 20 minutes | Makes 3¼ cups

Ingredients:

1½ cup	apple cider vinegar	½ Tbsp.	granulated garlic
1 cup	ketchup	½ Tbsp.	cumin
½ cup	brown sugar	1 tsp.	salt
¼ cup	Worcestershire sauce	½ tsp.	ground black pepper
2 Tbsp.	unsalted butter	½ tsp.	cayenne pepper
½ Tbsp.	onion powder		

Instructions:

Combine all ingredients in a saucepan and bring to a boil. Reduce heat and simmer for 10 minutes. Allow to cool and serve at room temperature.

RUB
Acapulco Pork Dry Rub
Total time: 10 minutes | Makes 3¼ cups

Ingredients:

1 cup	dark brown sugar	2 Tbsp.	chipotle powder
½ cup	granulated garlic	2 Tbsp.	sweet ancho pepper
½ cup	paprika	1 Tbsp.	chili powder
½ cup	kosher salt	1 Tbsp.	ground cumin
2 Tbsp.	granulated onion	1 Tbsp.	black pepper
2 Tbsp.	cayenne pepper	1 Tbsp.	dry mustard

Instructions:

Combine all ingredients in a mixing bowl and mix well. Use on ribs, pork loin and pork shoulder.

RUB
Backyard Beef Dry Rub
Total time: 10 minutes | Makes 2 cups

Ingredients:

¾ cup	paprika	2 Tbsp.	granulated garlic
¼ cup	ground black pepper	2 Tbsp.	garlic salt
¼ cup	kosher salt	2 Tbsp.	onion powder
¼ cup	sugar	2 tsp.	cayenne pepper
2 Tbsp.	chili powder		

Instructions:

Combine all ingredients in a mixing bowl and mix well. Use on beef brisket.

SEAFOOD

SAUCE
Saucy Citrus Scallops
Total time: 30 minutes | Makes 8 servings

Ingredients:

2 lbs.	scallops
½ cup	soy sauce
½ cup	orange juice
½ cup	honey
2 Tbsp.	citrus grill seasoning
2 Tbsp.	olive oil
1½ cups	calrose or jasmine rice
3 cups	water
2 cans	mandarin oranges (12 oz. each)
1 cup	crispy chow mein noodles
32 leaves	baby spinach

Instructions:

Thaw scallops per bag instructions. Set aside. Bring 1½ cups calrose or jasmine rice or any other fat, sticky, short-grain rice and 3 cups water to a boil and simmer, covered, for 20-30 minutes until fully cooked. While rice is cooking, combine soy sauce, orange juice, honey and seasoning in a small pot and mix until well blended. Place pot over medium-low heat and cook until reduced by half.

Heat oil in skillet over medium heat. Sauté scallops, approximately 4-5 minutes, until thoroughly cooked. Drain. Pour enough sauce over scallops to coat evenly. Reserve some sauce for garnishing.

Serve with rice, mandarin oranges and spinach. Garnish with noodles.

RUB
Ragin' Cajun Dry Rub
Total time: 10 minutes | Makes ½ cup

Ingredients:

2 Tbsp.	paprika	1 Tbsp	garlic powder
2 tsp.	cayenne	2 Tbsp.	onion powder
1 Tbsp.	salt	1 tsp.	oregano
1 Tbsp.	black pepper	1 Tbsp.	thyme

Instructions:

Combine ingredients in a small bowl and mix well. Coat seafood evenly and cook as desired.

MARINADE
Herb-Marinated Salmon
Total time: 30 minutes | Makes 8 servings

Ingredients:

8	salmon fillets
3 Tbsp.	lime juice
2 Tbsp.	olive oil
2 Tbsp.	parsley
1 tsp.	thyme
1 tsp.	black peppercorns

Instructions:

Before cooking salmon, be sure product is thoroughly defrosted by moving fillets to refrigerator for 8-10 hours, or immerse in cold water while still in packaging until defrosted, about 30 minutes. Combine lime juice, olive oil, parsley, thyme and peppercorns in a resealable plastic bag. Add salmon and marinate in refrigerator for 15 minutes. Preheat grill to medium-high heat. Remove salmon from the marinade. Grill each portion of salmon to the desired doneness, about 2-3 minutes per side.

BEEF

SAUCE
Cabernet-Mushroom Butter
Total time: 30 minutes | Makes 8 servings

Ingredients:

1 Tbsp.	unsalted butter
1/3 cup	onions, finely chopped
1/2 cup	portobello mushrooms, finely chopped
1 tsp.	minced garlic
1/2 cup	cabernet sauvignon wine
2 Tbsp.	fresh Italian parsley, minced
16 Tbsp.	unsalted butter, softened (2 sticks)
1 tsp.	cracked black pepper
1 tsp.	salt

Instructions:

In a heavy-bottomed saucepan, heat butter over medium heat. Add onions to pan and sauté for 3 minutes. Add chopped mushrooms and garlic to pan and sauté for an additional 5-7 minutes. Add wine to deglaze pan. Cook mixture until reduced, approximately 4-5 minutes. Remove from stovetop and let mixture cool. Once cool, add to softened butter. Mix in parsley and season with salt and pepper. Spoon butter mixture on top of grilled steak and let melt before serving.

RUB
Santa Maria-Style BBQ Rub
Total time: 40 minutes | Makes 8 servings

Ingredients:

1 tsp.	salt
1 tsp.	garlic powder
1 tsp.	sugar
1 tsp.	black pepper
1/2 tsp.	onion powder
1/4 tsp.	cayenne

Instructions:

Mix ingredients and rub on 3-4 lbs. tri-tip or top sirloin. Sear tri-tip on grill over high heat 2-3 minutes on each side. Move to indirect heat and cook an additional 25-30 minutes, turning occasionally, until beef is cooked to the preferred degree of doneness.

MARINADE
Dr Pepper®-Marinated Steak
Total time: 1 1/2 hours | Makes 4 servings

Ingredients:

4	steaks boneless, beef sirloin steak (8 oz. each)
2 cans	Dr Pepper® (12 oz. each)
2 Tbsp.	garlic, minced
3 Tbsp.	Mrs. Dash® seasoning

Instructions:

In a bowl, mix Dr Pepper and garlic. Add steak and coat evenly. Cover and refrigerate for 1 hour. Heat grill to medium-high. Remove steak from marinade. Discard remaining marinade. Sprinkle steak on both sides with Mrs. Dash seasoning. Grill steaks over medium-high heat for 3 to 4 minutes on each side or until desired doneness (160°F for medium).

CHICKEN

SAUCE

Citrus Chipotle Sauce
Total time: 45 minutes | Makes 2 cups

Ingredients:

1 Tbsp.	vegetable oil
½ cup	chopped onions
2 tsp.	garlic, minced
½ cup	sugar
¼ cup	lemon juice
1 cup	orange juice
¼ cup	lime juice
¼ cup	prepared barbecue sauce
½ Tbsp.	chopped canned chipotle chiles

Instructions:

Saute onions and garlic in oil for 10 minutes in medium pot. Add sugar, lemon, orange and lime juice. Cook over medium heat for 15 minutes. Add barbecue sauce and chipotle chiles. Cook on low for 5 minutes more. When cool enough, puree in blender. Serve over grilled chicken breast.

RUB

Moroccan Dry Rub
Total time: 10 minutes | Makes ⅓ cup

Ingredients:

1 Tbsp.	lemon pepper		½ tsp.	cayenne
1 tsp.	onion powder		1 tsp.	cinnamon
1 tsp.	garlic powder		1 tsp.	cumin
1 tsp.	salt		1 Tbsp.	sugar
1 tsp.	ginger			

Instructions:

Combine ingredients in small bowl. Rub on protein and grill.

MARINADE

Aztec Chicken
Total time: 30 minutes | Makes 4 servings

Ingredients:

4 ea.	boneless, skinless chicken breasts
¼ cup	apple juice
¼ cup	Bertolli® olive oil
1 Tbsp.	Tone's® taco seasoning
1 tsp.	cinnamon

Instructions:

Combine oil, apple juice, cinnamon and Tone's Taco Seasoning in a resealable plastic bag. Add chicken; marinate in refrigerator a minimum of 15 minutes.

Grill or pan fry chicken breasts over medium high heat until internal temperature reaches a minimum of 170°F or juices run clear.

PORK

SAUCE
Mango-Habanero Sauce
Total time: 30 minutes | Makes 3 ½ cups

Ingredients:

1 Tbsp.	vegetable oil
⅓ cup	chopped onions
2 tsp.	garlic, minced
2 Tbsp.	sugar
1 tsp.	habanero chili, seeded and chopped
2½ cups	mango, peeled and chopped
½ tsp.	salt
¼ tsp.	black pepper
¼ cup	fresh cilantro, minced

Instructions:

Heat oil in medium saucepan and saute onions for 2-3 minutes. Add garlic and cook an additional 30 seconds. Add sugar and chili. Cook an additional 1-2 minutes. Pour mixture into blender. Add mango, salt and pepper. Blend until smooth. Pour mixture into container and add cilantro. Serve over pork loin or chops.

RUB
Carolina Pulled-Pork Rub
Total time: 10 minutes | Makes 2 Tbsp.

Ingredients:

1 tsp.	salt
1 tsp.	garlic powder
1 tsp.	sugar
1 tsp.	black pepper
½ tsp.	onion powder
¼ tsp.	cayenne

Instructions:

Combine ingredients in a small bowl and mix well. Coat a 5–6 lb. bone-in pork shoulder evenly. To smoke pork, prepare your smoker per manufacturer's instructions. Smoke pork over low indirect heat for 8–10 hours.

MARINADE
Balsamic Rosemary Marinade
Total time: 10 minutes | Makes 2¼ cups

Ingredients:

1 cup	balsamic vinegar
1 cup	honey
2 Tbsp.	dry mustard
1 Tbsp.	rosemary garlic seasoning

Instructions:

Combine ingredients. Add to 4-6 pork chops; marinate in refrigerator a minimum of 2 hours. Grill pork chops over medium-high heat.

LAMB

SAUCE

Merlot Macadamia Sauce
Total time: 30 minutes | Makes 1 cup

Ingredients:

1 Tbsp.	olive oil
1 Tbsp.	shallots, chopped fine
1 tsp.	garlic, minced
1 cup	merlot wine (or red wine of your choice)
1 tsp.	cracked black pepper
1 tsp.	salt
2½ tsp.	fresh rosemary, minced
1 cup	beef stock
½ cup	macadamia nuts, chopped
2 Tbsp.	unsalted butter

Instructions:

In a heavy-bottomed saucepan, heat olive oil over medium heat. Add shallots to pan and sauté for 1 minute. Add garlic to pan and sauté for an additional 30 seconds. Add red wine to deglaze pan. Add pepper, rosemary and salt. Cook mixture for approximately 4-5 minutes. Add stock and bring to a boil. Reduce mixture to about 1 cup. Add butter and nuts to wine mixture and combine. Pour sauce evenly on grilled lamb chops and serve.

RUB

Garlic and Rosemary Frenched Rack of Lamb Rub
Total time: 20 minutes | Makes 8 servings

Ingredients:

2 lbs.	New Zealand® rack of lamb (16 chops)
3 Tbsp.	Spice Island® rosemary garlic
3 Tbsp.	olive oil
1 tsp.	Spice Island® Mediterranean Sea Salt
1 tsp.	Spice Island® black peppercorns

Instructions:

Cut New Zealand lamb racks into 1-bone chops. Sprinkle rosemary garlic, sea salt and black pepper evenly over lamb chops. Heat olive oil in sauté pan to medium-high heat. Sear both sides of lamb chops. Reduce heat and continue to cook for 8 minutes (until lamb reaches 140°F internal temperature), turning frequently. Serve immediately.

MARINADE

Lemon and Rosemary Marinade
Total time: 10 minutes | Makes 1 cup

Ingredients:

2 tsp.	Dijon mustard	¼ cup	olive oil
¼ cup	lemon juice	1 tsp.	salt
5 Tbsp.	fresh rosemary leaves	¼ cup	honey
2 cloves	garlic, minced	½ tsp.	black pepper

Instructions:

Combine ingredients. Add to 4-6 pork chops; marinate in refrigerator a minimum of 2 hours. Grill pork chops over medium-high heat.

Grilled Portobellos

Serve solo or as a side dish.

Recipe submitted by
Lyle Poulson
New Ulm, MN
Member since 2009

Total time: 50 minutes | Makes 4 servings

Ingredients:

4	portobello mushroom caps
⅓ cup	olive oil
2 tsp.	Spice World® minced garlic
¼ cup	balsamic vinegar
4	slices Monterey Jack cheese

Instructions:

Wash mushrooms and remove stems. In a resealable bag, combine oil, garlic and vinegar. Add mushrooms and let sit for 30 minutes. Remove mushrooms from marinade. Discard remaining marinade.

Preheat grill to high heat. Place mushrooms on grill, stem side down. Grill for 6-8 minutes on each side until tender and brown. Add sliced cheese to the tops for the last minute of cooking, and cook just until melted. Slice into strips and serve.

Light and Elegant Salmon Salad

Low-fat yogurt takes the place of sour cream for a salad that's lighter in fat but not in flavor.

Total time: 30 minutes | Makes 4 servings

Ingredients:

Dressing

¾ cup	cucumber, peeled, chopped, seeded
3 Tbsp.	plain low-fat yogurt
2 Tbsp.	lemon juice
1 ½ tsp.	fresh parsley, chopped
1 ½ tsp.	fresh chives, chopped
1 ¼ tsp.	grated lemon rind
¼ tsp.	black pepper
1 clove	garlic, minced

Salmon

4	C. Wirthy & Co.® salmon portions, thawed
1 tsp.	black pepper
½ tsp.	salt
	cooking spray or your favorite oil

Salad

4 cups	gourmet salad greens (about 4 oz.)
¾ cup	basil leaves
½ cup	ripe mango, cubed and peeled

Instructions:

Heat grill to medium-high.

For the dressing: While grill is heating, place dressing ingredients in a blender or food processor and process until almost smooth. Set aside.

For the salmon: Sprinkle salmon with salt and pepper. Coat grill with cooking spray (or other oil) and place salmon on preheated grill rack; grill 5 minutes per side or until salmon flakes easily when tested with fork. When done, break salmon into chunks.

For the salad: Place greens and basil in a large bowl; add ¼ cup of cucumber dressing and toss well. Arrange salad on 4 plates and divide salmon chunks evenly among plates; top each serving with 2 tablespoons of cucumber dressing and 2 tablespoons of cubed mango.

Grilled Caesar Salad

Hearts of romaine lettuce, gently grilled with homemade Parmesan croutons and creamy Caesar dressing.

Total time: 30 minutes | Makes 4 servings

Ingredients:

4	Taylor Farms® romaine hearts
12 oz.	Caesar dressing
6 oz.	Parmigiano Reggiano wedge
8	Parmesan croutons
3 oz.	extra virgin olive oil

Dressing

1	small tin anchovies
3 cloves	garlic large, peeled
3 oz.	red wine vinegar
2 Tbsp.	Dijon mustard
6 oz.	extra virgin olive oil

Croutons

1	sourdough baguette (sliced at an angle, ⅓" thick)
3 oz.	extra virgin olive oil
2 cloves	garlic, crushed
½ cup	shredded Parmesan cheese

Instructions:

Place the anchovies, garlic, vinegar and Dijon mustard into the bowl of a food processor, cover with the top and blend the ingredients until smooth. Slowly add the oil until thick and silky. Place in a separate bowl and store refrigerated until serving.

Preheat oven to 250°F. Using a pastry brush, lightly brush both sides of the angle-sliced croutons with the olive oil and garlic mixture, season with salt and pepper on one side and neatly arrange the croutons on a sheet pan. Place the pan in the oven for approximately 20 minutes or until light golden brown, remove the pan long enough to dust each crouton with Parmesan cheese and return the pan to the oven for approximately 10 minutes until the cheese has toasted.

Cut the romaine hearts in half lengthwise, exposing the full center of the lettuce heart. Brush each half of the lettuce with the olive oil and season with salt and pepper. Place the romaine hearts cut side down on a prelit grill over medium-low heat and grill for approximately 3 minutes or until the surface and leaves begin to char and gain grill marks. Flip hearts over and grill for another 2-3 minutes, depending on the heat. Remove the romaine from the grill and arrange on a large platter. Drizzle the romaine hearts with the cooled Caesar dressing and grind fresh black pepper over the top of the dressed lettuce. Using a vegetable peeler, shave the Parmigiano Reggiano over the top of the salad and garnish the platter with the Parmesan croutons.

Taylor FARMS

Cowboy Potato Packets

Chunky potatoes cooked in foil packets and topped with "the works."

Total time: 40 minutes | Makes 6 servings

Ingredients:

1 sheet	heavy-duty aluminum foil (24"x18")
1	medium onion, thinly sliced
4	medium potatoes (1½ lbs.), cut into ½-inch cubes
1 tsp.	seasoned salt
¼ tsp.	chili powder
¼ tsp.	ground cumin
1 can	chopped green chilies, undrained (4½ oz.)
1 cup	Kraft® shredded Mexican cheese
½ cup	Taco Bell® Home Originals® Thick 'N Chunky Salsa
½ cup	Breakstone's® or Knudsen® sour cream
¼ cup	chopped cilantro

Instructions:

Preheat grill to medium-high heat. Spray foil with cooking spray. Place onion in center of foil; top with potatoes. Mix seasoned salt, chili powder and cumin; sprinkle over potatoes. Top with chilies.

Bring up foil sides. Double fold top and ends to seal packet, leaving room for heat circulation inside.

Place packet on grill; cover with lid. Grill 30 minutes or until potatoes are tender. Open foil; sprinkle potatoes with cheese. Let stand 2 minutes or until cheese is melted. Serve topped with salsa, sour cream and cilantro.

Tip: For a great grilled meal, serve with grilled chicken breasts and a fresh fruit salad.

Kids' Ranch Pasta Salad

Healthy veggies cleverly disguised in a colorful toss of pasta, pepperoni and ranch dressing.

Total time: 30 minutes | Makes 8 servings

Ingredients

8 oz.	elbow macaroni
1 bag	frozen California blend vegetables (16 oz.)
8 oz.	mozzarella cheese, cubed or shredded
4 oz.	sliced pepperoni
½ cup	ranch dressing

Instructions:

Cook pasta according to package directions. Meanwhile, cook vegetables in microwave.

Mix all ingredients together in a serving bowl.

A&W® Root Beer Baked Beans

Make plenty! Everyone will want seconds on this side made with their favorite soda.

Total time: 50 minutes | Makes 6 servings

Ingredients:

5 strips	bacon, diced
1	large onion, diced
2 cans	baked beans (18 oz. each)
½ cup	A&W® Root Beer (not diet)
¼ cup	barbecue sauce
½ tsp.	dry mustard
	freshly ground pepper to taste
	several drops hot pepper sauce

Instructions:

Cook bacon with onion in a medium saucepan until bacon is brown and crisp. Add remaining ingredients. Heat to a boil; reduce heat and simmer, stirring often until slightly thickened. Transfer to an oven-safe baking dish and bake in the oven at 375°F for 20 minutes. Let rest 10 minutes and serve.

Cookout Corn

Buttery grilled corn makes a sunny side dish to your favorite meats and seafood.

Total time: 20 minutes | Makes 4 servings

Ingredients:

4 ears	corn on the cob
¼ cup	butter, softened (½ stick)
2 Tbsp.	Kraft® Grated Parmesan Cheese
1 tsp.	chopped fresh parsley

Instructions:

Heat grill to medium-high heat. Rinse corn under cold water; shake off excess. Wrap corn individually in foil. Grill 15-20 minutes or until corn is tender, turning occasionally. Meanwhile, mix remaining ingredients; spread onto corn after removing from grill.

Cherry Yum Yum

Cherry season is even yummier with this cool, creamy icebox dessert that's easy as pie.

Recipe submitted by
Janet Greer
and mother, Winnie Findley
Westminster, SC
Member since 1996

Total time: 45 minutes plus chilling time | Makes 8 servings

Ingredients:

1 box   graham cracker crust mix
2 pkg.   cream cheese (8 oz. each)
1-2 cups   powdered sugar
1 tub   Cool Whip® (8 oz.)

Cherry Pie Filling

5-6 cups   fresh pitted cherries, about 2½ to 3 pounds
½ cup   water
1¼ cups   granulated sugar
4 Tbsp.   cornstarch

Instructions:

For the pie filling: In a saucepan, combine cherries with remaining pie filling ingredients. Bring to a boil; reduce heat to low and cook, stirring frequently, for about 10 minutes. Cool before using in dessert.

Prepare graham cracker crust according to box directions in a round cake pan or 8"x8" glass baking dish. Cook, then cool completely. Cut cheese into blocks and beat with electric mixer. Fold in sugar. Add Cool Whip and mix. Spread over graham crust. Cover and chill in refrigerator overnight. Top with cherry pie filling and serve.

Fresh Strawberry Shortcake

A classic crowd-pleaser sure to impress friends and family.

Total time: 30 minutes | Makes 6 servings

Ingredients:

4 cups	fresh strawberries, sliced
½ cup	sugar
2 ⅓ cups	Bisquick® All Purpose Baking Mix
½ cup	milk
3 Tbsp.	sugar
3 Tbsp.	margarine or butter, melted
1 tub	frozen whipped topping, thawed (8 oz.) (or 1 can of whipped topping)

Instructions:

Mix strawberries and ½ cup sugar; set aside.

Heat oven to 425°F. Stir Bisquick mix, milk, 3 tablespoons sugar and butter until soft dough forms. Drop six spoonfuls onto ungreased cookie sheet.

Bake 10-12 minutes or until golden brown. Split warm shortcakes; fill and top with strawberries and whipped topping.

Tip: High Altitude (3,500-6,500 ft): Heat oven to 450°F. For shortcakes, decrease sugar to 1 tablespoon.

Light and Lemony Raspberry Bars

This low-sugar treat is loaded with luscious fruit flavor.

Total time: 1 hour plus chilling time | Makes 8 servings

Ingredients:

Filling

2 Tbsp.	all-purpose flour
1¼ cups	Splenda® No Calorie Sweetener, Granulated
½ cup	egg substitute
½ cup	half-and-half
½ cup	fresh lemon juice
1 Tbsp.	grated fresh lemon peel
¼ cup	reduced sugar raspberry preserves

Crust

¾ cup	Splenda® No Calorie Sweetener, Granulated
¾ cup	all-purpose flour
1	pinch salt
¼ cup	light butter

Instructions:

Preheat oven to 350°F. Spray an 8"x8" baking pan generously with butter-flavored nonstick spray. Set aside.

For the crust: Mix together flour, Splenda® and salt in a medium mixing bowl. Cut in light butter until the mixture is crumbly, like a streusel topping. Do not overmix. Press dough into prepared 8"x8" baking pan. Bake in preheated 350°F oven 15-20 minutes or until lightly browned.

For the filling: Place Splenda® and flour in a medium mixing bowl. Stir well. Add egg substitute and half-and-half. Stir until blended. Slowly add lemon juice while stirring constantly. Add lemon peel.

Stir raspberry preserves until they loosen up. Spread evenly over warm crust. Gently pour lemon mixture over preserves. Bake in preheated oven 20-25 minutes or until set.

Remove from oven and allow to cool before placing in refrigerator. Chill in refrigerator 2 hours before serving.

Cranberry-Oatmeal White Chocolate Chunkies

Classic oatmeal cookie studded with white chocolate and chewy dried cranberries.

Total time: 30 minutes | Makes 3 dozen cookies

Ingredients:

1¼ cups	Ocean Spray® Craisins® Original Dried Cranberries
⅔ cup	butter or margarine, softened
⅔ cup	packed brown sugar
2	eggs
1½ cups	old-fashioned oats
1½ cups	flour
1 tsp.	baking soda
½ tsp.	salt
⅔ cup	white chocolate chunks or chips

Instructions:

Preheat oven to 375°F.

Using an electric mixer, beat butter or margarine and sugar together in a medium mixing bowl until light and fluffy. Add eggs, mixing well. Combine oats, flour, baking soda and salt in a separate mixing bowl. Add to butter mixture in several additions, mixing well after each addition. Stir in Craisins and white chocolate chunks.

Drop by rounded teaspoonfuls onto ungreased cookie sheets. Bake for 10-12 minutes or until golden brown. Cool on wire rack.

Berry Delicious Angel Food Trifle

A trifle is an easy-to-make layered dessert made with cake, pudding, fruit or chocolate (or both!), and whipped topping. Feel free to improvise with your family's favorite flavors.

Total time: 30 minutes plus chill time

Ingredients:

1   30 oz. angel food cake
2   8 oz. containers whipped topping, divided
1   1.5 oz. package instant vanilla pudding, prepared according to directions on package
1   quart fresh strawberries, sliced, reserving a few whole berries for garnish*
1   pint fresh blueberries*
3   kiwi fruit, sliced*
    * Other berries or soft fruits can be substituted as desired

Instructions:

Cut angel food cake into 1"x 1" cubes using a serrated knife and set aside.

Toss all fruit together in a large bowl.

In a large bowl, gently fold together the prepared vanilla pudding and one container of the whipped topping.

Place a layer of angel food cake cubes in the bottom of a trifle bowl or punch bowl. Spoon a layer of the pudding mixture on top of the cake cubes. Top the pudding with a layer of the fruit. Repeat layers until all ingredients have been used.

Top trifle with the second container of whipped topping and garnish with the reserved whole berries.

Chill, covered, for at least 2 hours before serving. Store leftovers covered in the refrigerator.

Just Peachy Raisin Crostata

This Italian-inspired tart, perfect for casual company, is best served warm with vanilla ice cream.

Total time: 1 hour | Makes 8 servings

Ingredients:

1 cup	Sun-Maid® Natural Raisins
½ cup	sugar
2 Tbsp.	flour
½ tsp.	ground cinnamon
¼ tsp.	salt
4 cups	fresh peaches, peeled and sliced (4–6 medium)
	or 1 bag frozen peach slices (16 oz.)
1 Tbsp.	lemon juice
1	9-inch unbaked pie dough round or shell
	powdered sugar, for dusting (optional)

Instructions:

Preheat oven to 425°F. Place 9-inch round pie dough on a rimmed baking sheet. Combine raisins, sugar, flour, cinnamon and salt. Mix in the peaches and the lemon juice.

Mound the fruit mixture in the center of the dough, leaving a 1- to 2-inch border. Fold the dough up around the fruit mixture, gently pleating and pressing the dough against the fruit mixture.

Bake 10 minutes at 425°F; reduce temperature to 350°F and bake 20-25 minutes or until crust is golden brown. Some juices may seep out onto the pan. Cool on pan at least 10 minutes, or until juices have begun to set and crostata is cool enough to handle.

With a large spatula, carefully transfer crostata to a platter and dust with powdered sugar before serving.

Brownie Bite S'Mores

A classic campfire treat in a bite-sized morsel.

Total time: 15 minutes | Makes 8 servings

Ingredients:

4	graham crackers (whole)
8	brownie bites
8 Tbsp.	chocolate sauce
8	large marshmallows

Instructions:

Preheat oven to 350°F. Place 4 graham crackers on cookie sheet. Place 2 brownie bites on top of each graham cracker (side by side). Place 1 marshmallow on top of each brownie bite. Place in oven for 3 minutes, until marshmallows are melted. Remove from oven and carefully place graham crackers on plate. Drizzle each cracker with 2 tablespoons of chocolate sauce. Serve immediately.

Art Dessert

Oatmeal-Raisin Cookie Ice Cream Sandwiches

Two childhood favorites in one delicious dessert.

Total time: 45 minutes | Makes 12 sandwiches

Ingredients:

½ lb.	margarine or butter, softened (2 sticks)
1 cup	brown sugar, firmly packed
½ cup	granulated sugar
2	eggs
1 tsp.	vanilla
1½ cups	all-purpose flour
1 tsp.	baking soda
1 tsp.	ground cinnamon
½ tsp.	salt (optional)
3 cups	Quaker Oats®, quick or old fashioned, uncooked
1 cup	raisins
	softened ice cream or frozen yogurt

Instructions:

In large bowl, beat together margarine and sugars with electric mixer until creamy. Add eggs and vanilla; beat well. In medium bowl, combine flour, baking soda, cinnamon and salt. Add to margarine mixture; mix well. Stir in oats and raisins; mix well. Drop by rounded tablespoonfuls onto ungreased cookie sheets. Bake 10–12 minutes or until light golden brown.

Cool 1 minute on cookie sheets; remove to wire rack. Cool completely. Store tightly covered. To make sandwiches, spread softened ice cream on bottom side of one cookie; top with second cookie. Wrap airtight; freeze.

Baseball M&M'S® Cupcakes

Batter up! It's a breeze with these box-mix cupcakes topped with M&M's® candy.

Total time: 70 minutes | Makes 24 cupcakes

Ingredients:

1 box	yellow cake mix (18.25 oz.)
1½ cups	whipped vanilla frosting (12 oz.)
2 cups	M&M'S®
2	12-cup muffin tins
	paper cupcake liners

Instructions:

Preheat oven to 350°F. Prepare the cake mix according to the directions on the package. Line the muffin tins and fill each cup with ⅔ cup of batter. Bake for 20 minutes. Cool completely before spreading with whipped frosting.

Following the photograph, decorate the cupcakes with a single color of M&M'S to create the baseball seams.

Kaleidoscope Frozen Fruit Pops

A fruit-filled dessert that will brighten up your meal.

Total time: 1 hour 15 minutes | Makes 6 servings

Ingredients:

2 cups	colorful fruit, dried, frozen or fresh
2 cups	Mott's® apple juice
6	paper cups (6-8 oz. each)
6	craft sticks

Instructions:

Divide diced fruit among cups and fill evenly with apple juice. Place cups on level surface in freezer. Freeze until partially frozen, approximately 1 hour. Insert craft stick into center of each pop. Freeze until firm.

Sweet Basil Limonata

This refreshing herbal lemonade goes especially well with seafood, Italian and Asian cuisines.

Recipe submitted by
Jerry Semifero
Orange Beach, AL
Member since 1991

Total time: 15 minutes | Makes 8 servings

Ingredients:

2 cups	lemon juice, fresh-squeezed
1⅓ cups	simple syrup
2 cups	vodka (optional)
4 cups	club soda
½ cup	packed basil leaves (fresh, not dried)

Simple Syrup

2 cups	water
2 cups	sugar

Instructions:

Heat water and sugar until clear. Let cool. Lightly pack the large leaves and the small clusters of basil into a measuring cup until you have ½ cup basil leaves. In a pitcher, combine fresh-squeezed lemon juice, simple syrup, vodka and club soda. Hand crush the basil into the pitcher. Add ice, stir and enjoy.

Note: The basil flavor becomes more pronounced the longer it sets.

Strawberry ReaLemonade

Thirsty for something new? Try this refreshing twist on an old-fashioned favorite.

Total time: 5 minutes | Makes 8 servings

Ingredients:

1 qt.	fresh strawberries, cleaned and hulled
3 cups	cold water
¾ cup	ReaLemon® lemon juice from concentrate
¾-1 cup	sugar
12 oz.	Schweppes® club soda, chilled

Instructions:

In blender container, puree strawberries and 1 cup water. In pitcher, combine pureed strawberries, remaining 2 cups water, ReaLemon and sugar; stir until sugar dissolves. Chill. Add club soda just before serving.

Berry Lemonade Slush

Simple and refreshing for the whole family.

Total time: 15 minutes | Makes 8 servings

Ingredients:

⅓ cup   Country Time® lemonade-flavor drink mix (dry)
½ cup   water
3 cups   ice cubes
1 cup   fresh or frozen strawberries

Instructions:

Measure drink mix into blender container. Add remaining ingredients; cover. Blend on high speed 10 seconds. Turn off blender. Stir with spoon; cover. Blend an additional 5 seconds or until smooth, using pulsing action. Serve immediately. Store leftover slush in freezer.

Tip: Substitute blueberries or sliced peeled peaches for the strawberries.

Orange-Berry Blast Smoothie

The bounty of the season, blended into a thick and creamy drinkable treat.

Total time: 15 minutes | Makes 1 serving

Ingredients:

¾ cup	Tropicana® premium orange juice
1	medium peach, cubed
½ cup	blueberries
2 scoops	fat-free vanilla-flavored frozen yogurt
1 Tbsp.	crushed walnuts
1 Tbsp.	honey
1 cup	crushed ice

Instructions:

Place all ingredients in a blender container and blend until smooth. Pour smoothie into a large glass and garnish if desired. Each recipe makes one 10 oz. serving – double or triple the ingredients to make additional servings.

Blend together your perfect smoothie:

- Add more juice to create a thinner drink
- Use more fruit for a thicker texture
- Freeze your fruit for a chillier concoction
- Include a sugar substitute, molasses or maple syrup for a sweeter treat
- Get extra zing by adding more citrus juice
- Use fruit that's in season for fresher taste and more variety

Cape Cod Cosmopolitan

Relax with this fast and refreshing beverage.

Total time: 5 minutes | Makes 1 serving

Ingredients:

1½ oz.	vodka
	dash of orange liqueur
1½ oz.	Ocean Spray® cranberry juice cocktail
½ oz.	lime juice
1	lime garnish

Instructions:

In a cocktail shaker filled halfway with ice, combine all ingredients and shake well.

Strain mixture into a chilled stemmed cocktail glass. Garnish with lime twist.

Carolina Cooler

This refreshing cocktail with a southern twist provides a bit of "comfort" on a warm day.

Total time: 5 minutes | Makes 1 serving

Ingredients:

1½ oz.	Southern Comfort®
2 oz.	cranberry juice
½ oz.	orange juice
1	lime wedge

Instructions:

Fill a tall glass with ice. Add all ingredents and stir. Garnish with lime wedge.

Gentleman's Tea

Lend a dash of panache to your next patio party with this spirited twist on iced tea.

Total time: 5 minutes | Makes 1 serving

Ingredients:

1 ½ oz.   Gentleman Jack® whiskey
2 oz.   lemonade (not concentrate)
2 oz.   tea
          splash of lemon-lime soda
          lemon slice (for garnish)

Instructions:

In a mixing glass filled with ice, add Gentleman Jack, tea and lemonade. Stir contents, but do not shake.

Pour into a tall highball glass. Add a splash of lemon-lime soda. Garnish with lemon.

Lipton® Lemon-Sangria Iced Tea

(non-alcoholic)

Fast, refreshing and filled to the brim with the fruits of summer.

Total time: 5 minutes | Makes 8 servings

Ingredients:

½ cup	Lipton lemon sweetened iced tea mix
3 cups	cold water
2 cups	chilled grape juice
1	lemon, sliced
1	lime, sliced
1	orange, sliced
1	peach or nectarine, cut into chunks
2 cups	chilled club soda

Instructions:

Combine all ingredients except club soda in large pitcher; chill. Just before serving, add club soda.

Index

Index cont.

Index cont.

Acknowledgments

We'd like to extend our sincere thanks and appreciation to our outstanding culinary partners, exceptional food manufacturers and valued Members. Your talent, time and creativity gave this collection a very special flavor indeed.

Special recognition goes to our friends at the Kansas City Barbeque Society (KCBS), the world's largest organization of grilling enthusiasts. KCBS not only hosts more than 300 barbeque contests annually throughout America, it is actively involved in civic and charitable organizations that benefit from these events. Cookbook contributors Rod Gray, Troy Black and Mike and Debbie Davis are KCBS members as well as Sam's Club Members. Thank you for sharing your signature recipes for all to enjoy. For more information on the Society, visit www.kcbs.us.

- **Sam's Club® Kitchens**

Acknowledgments

Acknowledgments

Art Dessert

American Italian
Pasta Company

CSM Bakery Products